Also by Tash Aw

FICTION
The Harmony Silk Factory
Map of the Invisible World
Five Star Billionaire
We, the Survivors

STRANGERS ON A

TASH AW

Strangers on a Pier

PORTRAIT OF A FAMILY

4th ESTATE · London

4th Estate
An imprint of HarperCollins*Publishers*
1 London Bridge Street
London SE1 9GF

www.4thEstate.co.uk

HarperCollins*Publishers*
1st Floor, Watermarque Building, Ringsend Road
Dublin 4, Ireland

First published in Great Britain in 2021 by 4th Estate

Originally published as *The Face: Strangers on a Pier* in the
United States by Restless Books in 2016

1

Copyright © Tash Aw, 2016, 2021

Tash Aw asserts the moral right to be identified as the author of this work
in accordance with the Copyright, Designs and Patents Act 1988

A catalogue record for this book is available from the British Library

ISBN 978-0-00-842127-4 (hardback)

All rights reserved. No part of this publication may be reproduced,
stored in a retrieval system, or transmitted, in any form or by any means,
electronic, mechanical, photocopying, recording or otherwise, without
the prior permission of the publishers.

This book is sold subject to the condition that it shall not, by way of
trade or otherwise, be lent, re-sold, hired out or otherwise circulated without
the publisher's prior consent in any form of binding or cover other than that
in which it is published and without a similar condition including this
condition being imposed on the subsequent purchaser.

Typeset in Meridien by Palimpsest Book Production Ltd,
Falkirk, Stirlingshire

Printed and bound in Great Britain by CPI Group (UK) Ltd,
Croydon CR0 4YY

MIX
Paper from
responsible sources
FSC
www.fsc.org   FSC® C007454

This book is produced from independently certified FSC™ paper
to ensure responsible forest management.

For more information visit: www.harpercollins.co.uk/green

I

THE FACE

Pom mai ben Thai. Watashi no nihonjinde wanaidesu.
Jaesonghaeyo, han-guk saram ahniaeyo. Bukan orang
Indonesia. Ma Nepali ta hoina.

———————————

Ways to say what we are not, and to begin
the story of what we are.

ONE

I am in a taxi in Bangkok. My companion – European, white – speaks fluent Thai, but every time he says something the taxi driver turns to me with the reply. I shake my head. *Pom mai ben Thai.* I'm not Thai. *Not Thai.* He continues to address me, not my friend. I am the passive conduit for this strange tripartite conversation.

I am in Nepal, in the hills west of Pokhara. A village schoolteacher insists that I am a Gurung, an ethnic group of sheep herders and soldiers. I'm from Malaysia, I demur. You sure? Maybe your father was a Gurkha soldier who fought against the Malayan communists. Later, I stare at my face in a mirror for the first time in a week: my cheeks are rosy and sunburned from long days trekking at altitude, my eyes narrowed against the brilliant light. In my eyes, I look like a foreigner – or rather, like a local. Maybe I am a Gurung.

I am boarding a Cathay Pacific flight from Shanghai to Hong Kong. The Mainland Chinese attendants at the boarding gate bid me goodbye in Mandarin but twenty yards further on, the Hong Kong Chinese air crew waiting at the door greet me in Cantonese. (Most of the other ethnic Chinese passengers do not get this bifurcated treatment, I notice.)

It has to do with my face. My features are neutral, unpronounced, my skin tone changeable – pale in sunless, northern climates but tanning swiftly within a day or two of arriving in the tropics. My face blends into the cultural landscape of Asia: east of India, my identity becomes malleable, moulding itself to fit in with the people around me. Sometimes, I wonder if I aid this process unconsciously by adjusting my movements and behaviour to blend in; at a literary festival in Tokyo last year I realised that I was nodding respectfully as someone gave me directions in the street, when in fact I didn't understand a single word they said. I wonder if, on some level, I enjoy being mistaken for a local as much as I am frustrated that no one seems to know, or care, where I'm from. In some countries, like Thailand, where I can string a few basic sentences together, I find myself mimicking the local accent, which further confuses people. But it makes them happy, too. Same-same like Thai people, they respond cheerily when my identity is finally revealed. They draw their index finger around their face: my face is their face.

Same-same like me. Maybe it isn't to do with our faces, but with our wish for everyone to be like us. We want the stranger to be one of our own, someone we can understand.

TWO

Both my grandfathers lived on the banks of wide, muddy rivers deep in the Malaysian countryside, one on either side of the thickly forested mountain range that divides the country in two. One was a shopkeeper, the other a village schoolteacher. One lived in Perak, in a small town called Parit, not far from Batu Gajah, in turn not far from Ipoh, the state capital; the other had a more peripatetic existence, moving from a series of remote jungle towns – Tumpat, Temangan – before settling in Kuala Krai, in the heart of the Islamic state of Kelantan on the remote north-eastern coast of Malaysia. One was Hokkien, a *min-nan hua* speaker from Fujian province, the other from Hainan island, the southernmost territory of China, almost halfway down the coast of Vietnam and a mere few days by boat across the South China Sea to Malaysia.

(A quick aside: Hokkien, Hainanese; to these, add Cantonese, Hakka, Teochew. The differing regional roots of Chinese immigrants in South East Asia. Keep them in mind; they're important to this story.)

Both my grandfathers had, at some point in the 1920s, made the hazardous boat trip from southern China to the Malay Peninsula. They were mere teenagers when they made the voyage, fleeing a China ravaged by famine and fragmenting into civil war. I doubt their families would have known much about China's political confusion during the Warlord Era. They might have known that the Qing dynasty had recently come to an end, that they no longer had an emperor. But they would not have understood what it meant to live in the fresh ruins of a thousand years of Imperial rule, would not have understood the intricacies of the increasingly bitter conflict between Chiang Kai-Shek's nationalist Kuomintang and the swelling power of the Communist Party. They did not know they were living in momentous times, an era to end all eras, the beginning of a novel whose middle chapters we are only just approaching today. Theirs was a time that would set China on a course to dominate the world's imagination a hundred years later; but they would never see their country become the world's factory, the world's largest consumer of luxury goods, the world's second largest economy, respectful only of the might of the United States. In those few years, contemplating adulthood, they wanted only to escape crushing poverty.

And in those times the routes to salvation led, almost inevitably, to the warm, fertile lands that lay spread out across a vast archipelago south of China, where the Chinese emperors had established a centuries-old network of trading routes and an ancient relationship based on vassal and tributary states, with the ports of Singapore and Malacca at its epicentre. This was a place of promise, known to the Chinese as *Nanyang*, the Southern Oceans.

Sometimes, when I arrive in New York or Shanghai – old harbour cities that have drawn generations of immigrants – I find myself reimagining my grandfathers' arrival at the docks in Singapore, an unknown place whose sights and sounds must have been inexplicably comforting nonetheless. The temperature: hot and humid, exactly the same as the long summers of their homelands. There will be no cool season here, no brief respite from the heat and the rain, but they do not know this yet. The landscape: broad-leafed evergreen trees and waterways, the proximity of the sea. Again, much like home. The smell: of wet earth and rotting vegetation; of food, of possibility. But above all, it is the people who make them feel that they can live here. This is a British colony, but it is a city of free trade, then as now. Foreigners arrive easily, they find work easily; they stay. Built on eighty years of Chinese immigration since the establishment of British administration and the development of natural resources by the colonial government, Singapore is full of Chinese – labourers, dockside coolies, descendants of indentured workers in Malayan tin mines and plantations, but also merchants and tradesmen, artists, writers. There are Chinese newspapers, Chinese shops with Chinese signs painted in elegant traditional characters, Chinese schools, even a Chinese bank – the Overseas Chinese Bank. My grandfathers are not alone, and in fact, they are several generations away from being pioneers.

From here they seek out the person whose name and address they have been given. They keep it on a piece of paper, their dearest possession. All the other people on the boat have a similar piece of paper bearing the name of a relative, or maybe a person from their village who has left sometime in the past and established a home somewhere in Nanyang. But where to go, how to find these contacts? No one is sure of the geography of this foreign-but-familiar place yet; no one knows how far Kota Bharu is from Singapore, or whether Jakarta is closer to Malacca than Penang. Bangkok is somewhere north of here, but how far? They stand by the docks, figuring out where to go next.

Strangers, lost on a pier.

I think of this image often. For example, a few years ago, when I was in Morocco, speaking to a young man in Marrakech. He had no job and no hope of getting one. He wanted to go to New Jersey; he had an uncle there. The plan was to get to London, somehow, and then 'just . . . jump across' to America. Or the taxi driver I met last time I was in Jakarta, who thought Britain and the Netherlands must have been five, six hours away from Indonesia, and that maybe it would be good to get a job there. I told him the flight was fourteen hours long; he didn't believe me. He whistled and said, Fuck, you could get to Greenland in that time.

My grandfathers. Strangers lost on a pier.

Now, those regional identities – Hokkien, Cantonese, Teochew, Hainanese – this is where they are crucial to the new migrant from China. They are not about identity – not yet, anyway – but about survival. Their home village and the dialect they speak will ensure they don't perish in these new lands. Later, they will influence the direction of their new lives, and very likely those of their children, and perhaps even grandchildren too. For the person whose address they are now seeking is going to be a fellow Hokkien or Cantonese, someone who will provide them with a bed and food in the first instance, and then a network of contacts that will help them find a job. If they aren't true blood relatives, they will come to act as an extended family to the fresh-off-the-boat migrant. For the rest of their lives, these new arrivals will not forget their adoptive families, will not forget the kindness that was extended to them in those first days. *Uncle, Auntie* – this is what they will call the older members of the clan, a traditional Chinese practice carried on with particular zeal out here in Nanyang, so that two generations later, their grandchildren won't really know whether someone is an actual uncle or aunt, or just a stranger who once took in their grandfather.

Much later on, like the ramshackle houses they now live in, these large piecemeal clans will start to fracture and move on. There will be family feuds and people will start saying things like, we're not really even related to her. Families drift apart, their offspring marry and move to Canada, Australia, the States, and they no longer know how to address their elders, don't know which honorific title to use for someone one generation above or below them, can't speak the dialect that marked their clan as distinct, don't even know what Teochew food is, certainly can't place Xiamen on a map, and worst of all, can't read their own names in Chinese. They come back from college and greet a young uncle – not a true uncle but a generational one nonetheless, maybe someone who babysat the younger kids while the parents were out working – they will greet him with a casual 'hey dude'. They will probably convert to Christianity. Might even marry a Muslim. It will be a struggle to remind them that they're Hokkien, or Hakka, or whatever, and they will say it doesn't really matter, which is fine, now they are living in Sacramento, or Vancouver, or Melbourne, except that one day they will meet a white kid who's just graduated from Asian studies and spent a Junior Year Abroad in Beijing and asks them, So what dialect do you speak at home? And this kid talks to them in fluent Mandarin full of witty idioms they vaguely recognise as *chengyu*, those four-word aphorisms that hover, fog-like, on the edge of their consciousness. And suddenly their brains kick into automatic-translate mode, searching for the same words in Cantonese, only the meaning never emerges from the gloom and their heads are left in a real mess, constantly searching, searching like the spinning pizza of death that freezes the computer screen of their memory and doesn't give them the answers they need. They will think of Skyping their parents to ask, which will be awkward because frankly they've never made any attempt to speak the dialect, but now they have no choice because – guess what? – Google Translate doesn't do Teochew. So in the end they do call, but their parents don't answer, they're hopeless at technology, can't work their new iPads, and then *Game of Thrones* is on, and the moment is lost.

Still, though, that cloudiness remains in their thoughts, brooding, constant.

But for now, things are simpler. You know who you are, so you seek your own people; your kin, your *kakinang*, will help you. Find them, stick to them, and things will be OK.

Both my grandfathers must have had a name and address on a piece of paper. But who were these people? Who was the Hokkien guy who had given instructions to my grandfather, via friends or relatives, to make his way up the Malay Peninsula to the Cantonese-dominated town of Ipoh, nestled in a limestone valley pockmarked with tin mines? Who was the original *Hainamnang* who had set up home in a remote town on the edge of a jungle in the Islamic heartlands of the far north-eastern, where the Malay territory bled into Siam? We just don't know. Maybe the uncle of the grandfather of one of my childhood 'cousins', but maybe someone else – I'll – we'll have to ask.

It's always like this. I ask someone, they ask someone who asks someone else, but the response is always the same: we don't know.

THREE

I am sitting on the balcony of my parents' apartment in Kuala Lumpur, chatting with my father about his childhood. This is a rare occurrence. Not so much the chatting, though that is also a recent phenomenon, like an expensive luxury we have acquired in recent years, now that we are both older, less antagonistic. Gentle conversation between us, with no specific purpose or time limit, is something we are not yet fully accustomed to, something to be savoured only occasionally, and with great care.

What is truly precious in its rarity is his talking about the past – about *his* past. We are modern in our views, outwardly even westernised; but fundamentally, we are a traditional Chinese family, and this is no more clearly seen than in the way we interact with one another, in the things we reveal about ourselves. We do not admit weakness or sadness. Romantic heartbreak, depression, existential doubts – those are topics of conversation that belong to different cultures and younger generations, educated people who

14

know about Freud and psychotherapy and organic vegetables. Vulnerability is shameful, even taboo; and in the spectrum of human shortcomings, poverty is the greatest frailty. All that is broken must remain in the past.

The harnessing of the customary Asian characteristics of discretion and silence to suit a contemporary middle-class existence is what marks us as both traditional and truly modern inhabitants of Asia. For this is what happens all around us, not just in Malaysia but the whole of East Asia. Now that we are rich, we do not talk about the past; to study history is backward-looking, and we are only concerned with the future. Maybe this is how China deals with something as monumentally, catastrophically devastating as the Cultural Revolution, I suggest to my father. (I am skirting around the subject of his own past for the moment: talking about someone else's historic traumas might be a better way to broach the subject of his own life.) Perhaps the Cultural Revolution was so painful for the people who lived through it that it seems easier just to suppress memories of it, rather than digest all that it entailed, for unpacking all that baggage would fill their entire consciousness and leave them no space for anything else? So for them it's easier just to rejoice in the riches they have now, the handbags and apartments and travel and education and restaurants. The past is painful, the present is easy. It's a question of practicality: they just want to get on with their lives.

'No,' my father replies. 'It's not practicality. It's shame.'

His answer makes me pause. I'm not used to this direct-ness, especially since it seems to contain a confessional undertone, a prelude to greater openness. As a child, I used to wish that we could be more frank and touchy-feely with our parents, the way American families were in *The Cosby Show* and other programmes we saw on TV, but now I feel suddenly uncomfortable, as if I have intruded into a space that was better left unexplored. A part of me wants to reach for my iPhone and record what my father is about to say, but I don't, I just sit there, waiting; there is a fragility in the air.

My father tells me about his earliest memories – of growing up with distant relatives in those remote towns on the edge of the northern jungles while his father moved around the country searching for work and his mother lived elsewhere looking after his younger siblings. She didn't have the time or resources to look after him, the eldest of her four children, and he was by now just about old enough to live away from the family. He was seven, eight – no, nine, ten. He honestly can't remember.

What he can recall is being on a boat from Singapore – yes, it must have been from Singapore – up to Kelantan, the far north-eastern state where the family would settle. On the boat there were other recently arrived migrants from China but also India – Indian Muslims who performed their prayers and then shared their food with him. It was just some rice, but good rice, clean and white and nour-ishing, one of the best meals he can recall. He can remember my grandfather going away for weeks, maybe months, in search of work, can remember the time of brief abundance when my grandfather had a job and the family could afford to eat properly. He recalls the signwriting that my grandfather, a talented calligrapher, used to do as a sideline job to earn some extra money. For many years afterwards, they would pass black-and-gold signs that hung above certain shops and he would recognise my grandfather's elegant handwriting. He can remember, too, getting his first pair of shoes at the age of ten and feeling clumsy and heavy-footed. A few of these stories I have heard before; most I have not. He talks, also, about his half-sister, whom I knew but never well. As a girl, she was not deemed worthy of an education and was sent to work at the age of ten on the train between Malaysia and Thailand, where, urchin-like, she stole aboard and sold little packets of food to the passengers. My father would give her a lift up and she would prise open the window with a stick and clamber into the carriage – a plan that worked well until she slipped one day and speared her arm with the stick. This I did not know.

Listening to him, I am struck firstly by how free of resentment he is at his difficult childhood. His stories are not of a deprived-but-happy variety but neither are they full of the rancour you might expect of a person in his position. I remember, now, various conversations between him and his relatives – or, rather, members of the extended Kelantanese clan – on which I had eavesdropped without really meaning to as a child. Some of them, more open and talkative than my father, would discuss their underprivileged rural pasts with what I now recognise as a similar acceptance, a recognition that not everyone is born moneyed and comfortable. They are reconciled to society's lack of fairness – its hierarchy, if you like – because their stories are underpinned with a natural assumption that they will progress through its ranks:

They will be educated, to some degree.

They will become better off, even if never properly rich.

They will live and work in a big city.

Their children will become professionals and earn healthy salaries.

Their grandchildren will grow up so middle-class and affluent that the idea of deprivation will have no place in their lives, will seem to belong not to their country, but a much poorer neighbour like Cambodia or Bangladesh.

Like most migrants, my father and his Kelantanese clan have uncomplicated aspirations of education, work and upward mobility hardwired into their brains, which explains why America was their ideological Mecca; why I knew what SATs were when I was barely twelve years old and living ten thousand miles from the United States. Britain and the old countries of Europe might have been culturally interesting, but they were too obsessed with their past; the future was America (they could never have imagined the logic-defying rise of their miserable homeland).

'These are boring poor-people stories,' he interrupts

himself. 'They're not very interesting to you.' I demur, and press for more. Hearing him speak in such detail is rare and, frankly, a bit disconcerting, a bonding process that requires him to reveal more than I am accustomed to experiencing, like the time I was fourteen and he decided, in an awkward manner, to strip off entirely in the locker room after tennis, and we both had to pretend that we were comfortable with it. I suppress my urge to shrug and give up on the conversation, because while not yet on a roll, my father has been talking about things I've never heard of before, slowly stripping back the layers of memory, yet there's a lot more I want to know. We're still hovering on the periphery, I feel, still a fair distance away from knowing about my grandfather's first days in Nanyang. My grandfather died years before I was born, when my father was sixteen, and I have never really known anything about him beyond the basic facts of his life: that he had at some point been a village schoolteacher, was a skilful calligrapher, and in his latter years ran a coffee shop; that he died of throat cancer – he had been a smoker, too. Beyond this I know very little, nothing about his temperament, his idiosyncrasies, the little quirks that bring to life the human being behind the official portrait – not that it is a particularly well-drawn portrait in the first place, more like a sketch that has been blurred by years of neglect and left to grow damp so that even its outlines are obscured. This opacity has bothered me for as long as I can remember. But now my father stalls; he doesn't know what to say next. Our conversation falls into a sudden trough.

And in the silence, I begin to think: that's what frustrates me about a particular kind of migrant, the ones who drop their cultural baggage entirely in order to assimilate successfully into their new surroundings (as opposed to the other extreme, who cling desperately to memories of the homeland, and can't wait for the day they can retire and return to the place they have just left). For the problem with the Forgetters is that the need to wipe the slate clean in their adoptive country doesn't just begin and end with their arrival in their new land; it continues thereafter, repeating itself until it finds a convenient historical ground zero that is emotionally and intellectually untroubled, so that a new narrative about themselves is formed, a glowingly positive trajectory that strives for a clean story arc, complete with neatly packaged doses of pain – ultimately overcome, of course – that punctuate the rise to comfort and success and happiness:

We arrived from China, we were poor; we worked hard, and for a while our lives were difficult (but not really that bad); there were obstacles along the way, but look where we are now.

But how did you even get here? How did you end up in a godforsaken village on the edge of the jungle, where pet dogs got eaten by tigers – what chain of random decisions made you end up there? What were those 'obstacles', exactly? And all the silences, what did they hold? (I'm just wondering, because all throughout my childhood years, various close relatives spent long periods in hospital because they were ill, and one or two died from their illnesses and were rarely mentioned again, without any elaborate Chinese funerals to mark their passing, and it was only when I was in my thirties that I discovered that they had in fact been in psychiatric hospitals, squalid archaic institutions that treated mental illness as madness, and the ones who died had committed suicide; and I discern, too, that there is an abnormally high rate of mental health issues affecting the male members of my extended family, both the migrant branch in Malaysia and, historically, the ones who stayed in China – an abnormally high rate of suicide. So, I'm just asking.)

In the story of modern Asia, these messy blotches don't sit well with the clean lines of our reinvention. We apply them to national narratives, too, wiping out difficult relationships and entire periods of our history that make us feel uncomfortable because they disrupt the plotlines of our rise to middle class-ness, a status the World Bank calls 'upper middle income', soon to break into the realms of high income. In this story, minor conflicts of race, religion and class once existed but were swiftly overcome and no longer trouble us today; boundaries between countries that demarcated their cultural and ethnic differences were always in place, and provide justification for current nationalist arguments (there was never any overlap between these two territories, we were never, a mere few decades ago, the same people); there were violent riots in which many people died, but we have learnt from those lessons (no, there were never any *massacres*). History begins at a particular point and blithely skips a decade here, a half-generation there. Chinese people of any nationality talk endlessly about their history and heritage, make lavish films about it, but always, what they refer to is the ancient dynasties, a thousand or more years ago. One of the four great Chinese classic novels is *Romance of the Three Kingdoms*, set in a period ending in the third century. Everyone reads it at school, and there are at least seven feature films of it, plus countless TV adaptations. When history is that far back in time, it is safe and unthreatening. What happened thirty, forty, fifty years ago is another matter; that kind of history is more unsettling.

Always, the final act of this narrative involves the gratitude that accompanies the wealth of contemporary Asia. Look where we are now, compared to where we were not so long ago. This is intended to be both a justification for editing out those uncomfortable passages from our screenplay, and also a sort of closure, as if material comfort can provide the kind of finality that we need in order to live our lives happily.

But the problem with the official biopic is that it's boring. It is short on dramatic tension, despite the rocky moments that the person or the community or the entire country has to survive. It lacks intrigue because it is built on a careful logic that lacks silences, those shadowy unexplored areas that give us a fuller understanding of where we come from, how we are interlinked, where our futures lie. In simple terms, we need to know that messiness in order to know who we are.

My father is right. It is about shame. That is why we edit our stories the way we do, to alter our image not just for others but for ourselves. In Kuala Lumpur and Ho Chi Minh City and elsewhere in South East Asia we rename all the streets so that they bear names of our national heroes rather than the names of the Scots and Englishmen and Frenchmen who once colonised us. The act of reclaiming one's national heritage is necessary, and inevitable, but it is nonetheless about shame – the shame of having been colonised, of having been the subject of a distant monarch, of having answered to someone stronger and richer. Poverty means frailty, and it is shameful, even now that we have skyscrapers and high-speed trains. We can't live, comfortably or uncomfortably, with the knowledge that our story was narrated by someone else during those long early chapters, so we edit those passages out. But, as any storyteller knows, the editing process is addictive – buried in the mess there is a perfect story waiting to emerge – so we chisel away obsessively, chipping off entire blocks from the structure, more and more and more, until finally we have an unblemished, featureless mass. This is the form that pleases us.

But consider what happens when you get into a cab in Penang, for example, and ask for Lebuh Leith, which has been called Lebuh Leith on official maps for as long as I can remember, and the driver says, 'Oh, you mean *Leith Street*.' Somewhere beneath the polished surface of our narrative, the messiness still remains; we carry it with us, unexpressed, unacknowledged. The divisions and conflicts of the past remain inside us too, the unexamined, unprocessed trauma, seeping into the way we organise our societies.

This is why the story of how my grandfather came to settle in the depths of Kelantan is important to me. This is why I am here with my father, sitting through the awkward silence and resisting the urge to go and get another soda for myself and a cup of tea for him, or refill the bowl of groundnuts we have been sharing, or check my iPhone for messages, or something else that will relieve the suddenly stilted atmosphere but also put an end to our unexpectedly frank conversation. Somehow, I feel his story might help explain why my face is becoming more angular as I grow older, shedding the chubby cheerfulness that I had throughout my childhood, that comes from my mother's family. It might explain why I can pass for anyone, anywhere in South East Asia; might explain why no one ever guesses where I'm from. But something has happened – maybe I've asked one question too many, maybe I've touched a nerve, maybe my father regrets having told me so much.

We contemplate the view of the city in the distance, the Twin Towers rising from a base of smaller high-rises. There is no smog today; from our suburb a few miles away, the city centre looks impossibly snug in the Klang Valley, protected by the mountain range beyond. In this light, the hills look almost blue. A strong breeze starts up, blowing some groundnut shells off the table. My mother is calling from inside the apartment. Still, I wait.

FOUR

A monsoon-season downpour: the rain falling so heavily that the view from the classroom windows has become shrouded in a pearly-grey mist. The sports fields and the line of acacia trees on the perimeter is fuzzy, their outlines uncertain – a watery mirage. Next to the classroom there is a corrugated zinc roof that shelters the canteen; the rain clatters onto it so loudly that it's difficult to hear ourselves speak. In class, the lesson has been cancelled. Heavy rain, lightning, a power cut – it's too dark to read. Best of all, our teacher isn't here, kept away from school like half of the class by the occasional drama of the rainy season: *banjir*. Floods, not just in the *kampung* – 'urban villages' that are in truth little more than slums – but in the suburbs, on the highways: everywhere, the colour of milky tea, swirling knee-deep, threatening foolhardy motorists with water-logged exhaust pipes, turning the deep monsoon drains into frenzied torrents that will, in the days to come, yield at least a couple of tragic stories – small children playing next

26

to these impromptu city rivers slip into the currents and are carried away to their deaths. Growing up in Kuala Lumpur, even in a gentrifying suburb, we have a sense that death is never far away.

Inside the classroom, the wind is sweeping the rain through the louvre windows which are old and stuck and won't close, so we've shuffled the wooden desks towards the middle of the room. The substitute teacher – a young recent graduate from teacher training college, huddles over a book, looking up with decreasing frequency to check that we are under control. She is engrossed in her novel, which someone later claims to have spotted, despite her attempts to hide it within the pages of a geography textbook – a torrid bodice-ripper with a swooning woman, one of those Mills & Boon paperbacks that girls from the convent school next door are starting to buy at the second-hand bookstores in the nearby cluster of shops in State, opposite the central car park square where one of our classmates was recently spotted smoking *during* school hours. We are fifteen years old, and life is about to change for us.

This is the year we take our first major public exams, the *Sijil Rendah Pelajaran*, or Lower School Certificate, which every pupil of our age in a publicly funded school will sit. When the results are published nationally, there will be articles in the newspapers about students who have overcome disabilities or extraordinary setbacks in their family circumstances to excel in the exams, stories about village schools with an unusually high number of A-grade students – tales

that fit nicely into our growing modern narrative of achievement and transformation. Personal success that takes place
on a national scale: this makes us feel that we are all changing
for the better. But away from the limelight, there will be a
more important shift, for we will begin to articulate, with
almost adult awareness, the differences in class, money and
privilege that exist between us.

As pupils in a public secondary school in Malaysia in
the 1980s, we have, up until now, lived in a state of happy
ignorance. The teaching is earnest but ineffective. Our
classes are too big, and most of the forty-five boys in each
class are too distracted by football or music to be serious
about work, so the atmosphere during lessons is relaxed,
the teachers resigned to their role as idle shepherd, watching
over a flock that just wants to do its own thing. We are in
an old Catholic school now run by the government,
although among the teachers there are still one or two
Salesian Brothers, missionaries and teachers whose tropical-
white robes cut an increasingly strange figure in a country
whose national identity is growing stronger with each year.
Its economy is growing, too, and we are riding its optimism.

We are ignorant, most of all, of the divisions that exist
between us. We live in a country governed by racial politics,
but in school this doesn't seem to matter. It's true that there
are unofficial cliques that seem to be dominated by one
racial group or another – Chinese boys play basketball,
Indian boys play hockey, and the school football team is
dominated by Malay rocker boys who cut out pictures of

Metallica from magazines and stick them to their textbooks. But in class and during breaks, the racial mix is an easy blend of skin colour and language, a patois of English, Malay and Cantonese. We don't notice, at this stage, the fact that we come from different family backgrounds too. There are boys whose names bear the prefixes Raja or Tengku that mark them as being from the various royal families; there are those like me, who live in aspiring middle-class suburbs nearby; there are boys who come from poorer rural areas, who live in hostels subsidised by the Ministry of Education; there are those whose parents work as janitors and dishwashers. In my year there is a boy called Mahendran, who writes with difficulty, and whose rubber-tapper parents are illiterate (they are not the only ones). There are pupils with learning disabilities, who nonetheless appear at school every day but merit no special attention from the teachers. There are the geeks who excel at math (usually Chinese), as well as small-time gangsters who get into fights after school and occasionally get expelled (usually Chinese); but generally we blend into a single mass that coasts along without drama. We spend time together at breaktime, are at least cordial to each other, are ignorant of just how deep the divisions are between us.

We are here because we are all children of the underprivileged, people who have known, to some extent or another, deprivation. Who were not born into a country that had ever produced a bourgeoisie. Who measure themselves against the countries of the West, with their generations of middle classes and education and stable government. Who want the same thing, now, for themselves and their children. Who believe they will achieve the same stability and wealth and high culture in their lifetimes. We are here because we are part of a process of nation-building, because our parents believe in a common project of construction – of the self, of the society, of the country – that is based on improvement, the constant onward drive of the narrative of modernity. We do not know this, at our age, but we are all part of the way we are telling the story of ourselves, to ourselves.

But in less than a year, when – like all the other fifteen-year-olds in our twenty-five-year-old country – we contemplate the results of our public exam, we will begin to see, with startling clarity, how our parents have not been deprived in quite the same way, how their ambition has been played out differently in merely half a generation. We will see how our paths are not just pulling us apart but accelerating our journeys, placing some on an elevator to super-achievement, others on a broken-down staircase. For when the results are published, we will be measured against each other brutally, and we will discover some surprising things about each other. Some kids, it turns out, have been doing advanced trigonometry with their architect parents. Some kids have been reading Steinbeck and writing short stories in their spare time. Someone else went on a geology field trip to Sumatra with a bunch of adults. We had never realised what each other's parents did for a living until now, never known what their jobs meant – for them or for us.

Now, the brightest students from modest backgrounds are applying for scholarships to schools in Singapore, which has the best high school grades in the world; in a few months, they will be gone. Now, the not-so-bright kids from the richest families will be sent to finish their high school in boarding schools in England, their families panicking, suddenly, about the quality of the education they are receiving in our school. They, too, will not come back next year. Now, we have become aware of schools elsewhere in the world where fees cost ten times the average annual salary in Malaysia, and we realise that for some of our families – families we had previously assumed were more or less the same as ours – such fees are affordable. Now some of our older siblings are starting to win scholarships to universities overseas, and for the first time, we hear names such as Oxford or Harvard or the National University of Singapore.

And then there are the rest, the huge majority who will stay for another two, maybe four years before either trying to get into university or to get a job. For those who have done well in the recent exams, the swift departure of some of our friends for greener pastures has driven home the reality of Higher Education; for those who have barely scraped through, the sudden obsession of their erstwhile friends with getting into university seems to be more and more bizarre. The two camps begin to detach from each other, one withdrawing into a world of algebra and increasingly complex sentence structures, the other into heavy-metal bands and football, Cantopop and petty crime. And within the group destined for higher education there are marked differences, too: there are those who study with the sort of desperate intensity that indicates their families' modest backgrounds – they *must* win scholarships, somehow, somewhere – and those who go about their business with an easy insouciance, reading novels that aren't required for class and bringing up first-hand experience of travel to Japan or Australia during geography lessons; their families are better off, perhaps not rich but comfortable enough to give them help if they don't gain the top grades. In just one year, we have divided, and subdivided ourselves, and it is class, not race, that has created this schism. In just one generation, we have created a society of hierarchy.

In this long vacation after the end of the exams, we drift slowly apart, drift through the long rainy days that we spend cycling through suburban lanes or fishing in the small ponds and streams that nestle in the pockets of jungle that still exist in our neighbourhoods. We take the bus that meanders down to the coast, where the sea is mucky and brown and the beaches strewn in twigs and casuarina leaves, and where the days and night seem even longer because there is even less to do. When we go back to school we will be in Form Four, the penultimate year of obligatory schooling, the year before the next public exams that will definitively open or close the doors to the rest of our lives. When we go back to school, we will find that one of our classmates had been driving with his small-time gangster friends down to Port

Dickson at the same time we were on the bus heading down there, singing to our Walkmans in the back row; we will learn that he had been driving too fast, driving illegally (for we are not quite sixteen); that he might have been drinking; that the car crashed; that he was the only one in the car who died. He had been a talented badminton player in primary school; I remember him at age ten or eleven, swift and elegant; now he was dead. In the canteen, there will be talk by his friends of avenging his death, of finding out who exactly it was who had given him the whiskey and car keys and beating the fuck out of that guy.

The ones doing the talking will have come back to school with their hair dyed orange, their voices louder and filled with hardcore Cantonese slang, delivered without the play-fulness of before, every sentence containing the words FUCK, MOTHER and CUNT. They get into shouting matches with the male teachers, threaten to burn their cars, and even in class they whistle at the young female teachers. They don't care about rules now. The results of the exams will have made them feel that nothing matters. But for those in the other camp – suddenly, there is a huge, glaringly obvious other camp – *that* kind of talk, *those* people (we now refer to each other as foreign entities) are irrelevant, and soon won't even figure in our universe of books and application forms and SATs and TOEFL and UCCA. We are sixteen, seventeen. There is open enmity. The wannabe gangsters pick on the occasional nerd and extort money from him for a few months with threats of violence. *We know where you live. We know where your sister goes to school, we gonna rape her.* Standing out in any way is not good news. In my case, it was my face – round, slightly cherubic, totally free of teenage acne – that gets me, rather than any academic prowess. I hand over my pocket money – laughably modest sums, in retrospect – on a monthly basis, for several months before a deal is struck on my behalf by a friend, a rare bourgeois gangster, accepted on both sides of the divide, who arranges a purchase of some cigarettes as final payment. A couple of years later, celebrating a friend's admission to Stanford, some friends and I will find ourselves in a fast-food joint late one evening. There, in a brown uniform and comically origami-like hat, will be my principal extortionist, a boy older than us who'd dreamt of being a big-time *tai-kor* gangster, who'd boasted about slashing someone in the face while he was still at school. He will recognise me, and lower his eyes when he asks, Do you want fries with that? And I will not know why, but I am the one who feels embarrassed, almost guilty.

The end of the 1980s is in sight; soon there will be huge American-style shopping malls selling Nike Air sneakers in Kuala Lumpur; we already have McDonald's and Wendy's and Kentucky Fried Chicken. In less than a decade we will have bars on the rooftops of skyscrapers selling Stolichnaya and Bollinger, French restaurants serving pan-fried foie gras, nightclubs with trance DJs from Germany and cheap ecstasy pills from Thailand, a dizzying cocktail of drugs and money so intense that forty-year-old investment bankers will die every month of heart attacks on the dance floor. Then, as now, death is never far away in Kuala Lumpur. But that life will be reserved for a select few, those among us who are detaching themselves and forming an exclusive class within a class within a class, so that in ten years, when we are only in our mid-twenties, our paths could never cross again, not even in a fast-food joint. We don't know that yet, but we will, very soon.

FIVE

Whenever I am in China, the question I'm most frequently asked – by taxi drivers, waiters, shop assistants, people with whom I've fallen into casual conversation – is 'where are you from?' by which they mean not only which country I'm from, but which regional group I am descended from, which dialect my family speaks at home. In Hong Kong and Taiwan, passing conversations about travelling – about destinations and origins – lead eventually to the same question. In Singapore, where the large and long-established immigrant Chinese communities identify strongly with their regional ancestry, people simply ask, 'Are you Hokkien?' (though mostly they just presume I am).

For most people unfamiliar with China and its culture – and by that I mean the societies and customs of the mainland and the Overseas Diaspora – the most prominent assumption is that of homogeneity, of a huge mass of people who look, think and behave in largely the same way. The threat of this single-minded, single-willed horde of billions exerting its collective ambitions on the rest of the world is what fuels the imagination of economists and politicians today. The Chinese government happily promotes this idea, this image of One China consisting of a monocultural country inhabited overwhelmingly by one racial group, the Han Chinese who account for over ninety per cent of the population of the People's Republic, and nineteen per cent of the world's population. And in many circumstances, Chinese people themselves, whether born in Beijing or Hong Kong or Ipoh, presume a certain familiarity with one another, as if tied by an ancient kinship that defies nationality. But when you get down to the detail, once you get past the pleasantries and start talking about yourself, all Chinese people want to know is where you're from, how you're different from them.

This is hardly surprising given that China is in fact a continent all on its own, almost as big as Europe and rich with dramatic geographical and cultural variety. Someone from the extreme north of China does not belong to the same cultural or linguistic grouping as someone from the extreme south or west; they don't share the same customs, language, food, dress, climate – all they have in common is Mandarin, the national language that all of the fifty-six recognised ethnic groups are taught at school, the language of government and commerce. But at home, where we develop our sense of ourselves, where we become aware of who we are and what we stand for, every Chinese person speaks their own dialect. When I lived in Shanghai, I was struck by how extensively the local dialect was used, and how incomprehensible it was to most other Mandarin speakers. Locals were proud to speak it, proud that it defined them against Beijing. But that was only one of the many identifiable dialects I heard while I lived there. On the borders of the Shanghai Municipality lies the small, prosperous province of Zhejiang, whose capital Hangzhou boasts the picturesque West Lake and China's first Apple Store, among other attractions. There, in the favoured weekend destination of Shanghai dwellers, I heard dialects I later found to be markedly differing variations of the Wu language of Zhejiang. Hangzhou, Shaoxing, Ningbo, Wenzhou, Taizhou, Quzhou: every city nestled in a valley within the province had its own distinctive dialect. These relatively small differences are nonetheless noticeable, nonetheless worthy of further inquiry; so imagine these differences applied to a whole continent and an entire diaspora, whose people look vaguely similar, share broadly similar biological DNA, but whose lives are vastly different in every other respect?

It's no wonder that the Chinese are experts in the vocabulary of classification, in the art of distinguishing one group of people from another. Americans of any ethnic or regional heritage who meet abroad tend joyfully to introduce themselves as 'American'; Chinese people have to establish whether they are *Zhongguo ren*, *Hua ren*, *Huaqiao*, *Huayi* – the most common denominations of nationality and cultural background in standard Mandarin. Partly this has to do with having a large, old diaspora, which invites the subcategorisation of ethnic Chinese according to place of birth, country of current abode, length of time spent in that country, and whether they are there temporarily or intending to return to China. Everyone and everything is defined in relation to *Zhongguo*, the Middle Kingdom.

Often, there is a sense of belonging to a greater fabric of Chineseness which defies nationality and goes some way to explaining the assumptions of familiarity that Chinese people make all the time: 'You may sound American and dress like a skateboarder, but still, we understand you because you *look* Chinese.' The truth is, though, that these superficial similarities rarely mask the differences that ethnic and culturally Chinese people draw between themselves. Chinese people might define themselves as an amorphous but vaguely homogenous group in the presence of a third, more foreign presence, but among themselves, divisions are real and ever-present. The recent protests in Hong Kong started out as political, but they soon became a battle of culture, a fight to define a local identity with the speaking of Cantonese at its heart. I've been to Hong Kong three times in the last year; each time, I've found a widespread and noticeable reluctance to speak Mandarin, especially among the ordinary people who drive taxis and buses and wait tables. My bad Cantonese was received with warmth, my good Mandarin with thinly disguised resentment.

The reality is that China, and being Chinese, involves dizzying, often exhausting variety; to travel in China and the Chinese countries of East Asia is to make the same cultural and linguistic leaps as one makes on those student backpacker trips by rail through Europe. The people might look the same, but they are different. In countries such as Singapore and Malaysia, where the old, pre-revolution communities have not been subject to the homogenisation of Communism, such divisions are even more marked, even celebrated. Temples and clan associations serve their own communities and bear names that mark them as Hokkien, Teochew, Cantonese or Hakka. They were the original establishments that provided support for those waves of migrants, lost on a pier. So strong were those bonds that jokes that rejoice in cultural divisions are still made today. *Of course he's a gangster, he's from Chaozhou. I knew it, she has a Hokkien face. That whole company is dominated by Hakkas, they look after their own people.*

For people in the West, such distinctions are totally irrelevant. I rarely bother explaining the cultural differences between a northerner and a southerner, between a Hokkien and a Cantonese; it's hard enough explaining the fact that I'm Malaysian *and* Chinese. It's usually slightly easier to communicate this basic distinction to other people whose nationality and ethnicity are not conveniently unified. A British person of Pakistani parentage is more likely to understand what I mean when I talk about Singaporean Chinese or Cantonese clannishness in Hong Kong than, say, a Franco-French Gaul.

Often, I give up when I feel the explanation of where I'm from and who I am might seem too complicated.

Sometimes I just pretend to be whatever someone assumes I am. Sometimes I am from Shanghai. Sometimes I'm from Taiwan. Sometimes I'm Muslim (because I'm Malaysian). If I could speak Japanese I'd be tempted to be from Kyoto. Temples, *sakura*: such a picturesque backstory.

SIX

I speak Mandarin with a neutral accent but my speech inevitably bears traces of my origins and education, of growing up in a household where my parents spoke to each other in the Minnan dialect of Fujian province (specifically with a Penang-Malaysian accent and vocabulary), to us in Mandarin, to their siblings in Hainanese (on my father's side) or a mixture of Hokkien and Cantonese (on my mother's side). At school in Kuala Lumpur, a city historically dominated by immigrant Cantonese-speakers, the only Chinese language I used was Cantonese, mainly of a slangy, coarse variety that consisted mostly of profanity; otherwise I studied in and spoke Malay and the local strain of English. With my cousins in rural Perak and Kelantan I spoke a pidgin of Malay, Mandarin, English and Cantonese. I became quite skilled, quite young, at modulating my speech to suit whomever I was speaking to. I knew what proportion of Malay or Mandarin or colloquial English to use, and in what situation, knew when to swear in Cantonese, knew when to be correct, when to be urban-cool, when to be country-direct.

In a country like Malaysia in the 1980s – multicultural, rapidly urbanising, rapidly creating a wealth-based class system – you learn to switch linguistic and cultural codes. In our suburb on the border of Kuala Lumpur and Petaling Jaya, its principal satellite town, virtually everyone had close relatives who still lived in the countryside; now, one generation later, most of those extended families will have moved into the cities.

I spent most of my school holidays with my maternal grandparents who lived in a 1920s shop-house in a small town called Parit, in the heart of the tin-mining region of Perak. It was a happy, generally uncomplicated existence: my grandfather spoke only Hokkien and Malay; my grandmother (his second, local-born wife) spoke Hokkien, Malay and exceptionally good English. They lived in the house with my uncle and aunt and their children, a large Chinese family in a largely Malay area. My relatives on this side of the family had an often-told, comfortably messy history. I knew where they were from, heard stories about my grandfather's early days in Malaysia, knew how he met my grandmother. Towards the end of her life, she – unusually for a woman of her generation – told me how she felt about my grandfather, told me about her doubts about marriage and of wanting to flee, which of course she would not have done, as it would have been impossible;

43

yet she had thought about it. It was a family whose past and present felt resolved – far from perfect, yet allied to a time and place that gave them a solid, rooted identity. And so I, too, wanted to fit in, wanted not to be seen as a prissy urban dweller who didn't know the ways of the country. I helped out in the shop – the kind of general store in a small town that sold school uniforms, soap, underwear – and pretended to be one of them. When old Malay ladies came into the shop to buy talcum powder, I affected a local accent, dropping all traces of city slang; when hanging out with my cousins I changed my cultural references, picking up on the same shows and music they were into (not the same as the ones my friends back in KL enjoyed).

But all along, I was plagued by a sort of anxiety, a low-level fear of something I couldn't articulate until I was in my twenties: the knowledge that I was an imposter, that I would, at any time, be revealed as an outsider. A precious city boy. A nerd. A snob. Someone alien to his own family. I worried that they'd look at me and think that I wasn't one of them; and that would be awkward, for them and for me, because most of the time, I was definitely part of the family. What to do, then, with the sudden appearance of a stranger at the family table? By the time I was in my mid-teens and reading long novels, sustaining the right kind of vocabulary and slang in the countryside became harder and harder. The ideas in my head started to seem impossible to express with the language I knew I had to use to fit in – and occasionally I would let slip a word that betrayed me, revealed me as a fraud. (Once, when we saw a section of jungle that had been cut down to clear space for a growing palm oil plantation, I talked about *deforestation*). I read Faulkner and Steinbeck in private, hiding the books between the clothes in my bag. My sister, older, tougher, more determined to escape, openly practised Chinese calligraphy and French grammar in the shop, ignoring the customers who came in to buy a box of sewing needles and chat about the level of the river during the recent rains. She had staked her claim to a separate existence, was pursuing it honestly and single-mindedly. She was still in the shop, still speaking Hokkien and Mandarin, but her life was already detaching from that of our cousins and grandparents, like a slowly shifting tectonic plate breaking off to form its own continent.

The unease we felt was about the privileges we had – the education and opportunities that were making us drift apart from the rest of our family – but more precisely, it was about money and class and guilt. That was what none of us could say, for perhaps we couldn't articulate it back then, when it was not yet clear just how an education could change our lives, when we did not yet know, in real practical terms, how a degree from Cambridge would make you a fundamentally different person from someone who shared your bloodlines and DNA but who quit a rural Malaysian school aged seventeen. The awkwardness we felt came from the same place as that which arises between me and my father when I ask him about his childhood: I want to be somehow part of his past, to be a part of his formation, but I can't. The education I have had has made it impossible for me to go back there.

I remember reading, for the first time, Alice Walker's essay about Cuba, and about her relationship with her father. I remember reading and re-reading and thinking it had been written just for me: 'This brilliant man . . . but unschooled beyond the primary grades . . . found the manners of his suddenly middle-class (by virtue of being at a college) daughter a barrier to easy contact, if not actually frightening. I found it painful to expose my thoughts in language that to him obscured more than it revealed.' The essay's title, 'My Father's Country is the Poor', stayed in my head for days, haunting me in ways I couldn't explain. I wasn't African-American, not impoverished, and yet I thought I had been reading about myself.

I also remember this: we are in my grandfather's shop; he is writing numbers in a ledger and occasionally making small calculations on the abacus. I am arranging the coal-tar soap in neat rows on the shelves nearby, trying to appear uninterested in the conversation I'm overhearing. My mother is dusting the glass tops of the cabinets with a feather duster, as she must have done all throughout her growing-up years; and she is telling my grandfather about my sister ringing the week before, in tears, from Singapore. She had won a valuable Singaporean government scholarship and was now living with a bunch of other fifteen-year-olds

46

in a dorm nearly two hours' bus ride from Raffles Girls' School, where she was receiving the kind of education my parents had always wanted for her. When we had visited the dorm, even my father, hardened as he was to a Spartan childhood, had said, simply: It's not very nice. Now she was homesick, lonely, studying crazy long hours just to keep pace with the most driven teenagers in South East Asia. Straight As every year or you lose your scholarship. She wanted to come home.

My grandfather makes a funny noise – something like a laugh, only it doesn't sound at all jolly. He is unmoved by this, finds it ridiculous. He had come to Malaysia as a boy with nothing but the shirt on his back; he doesn't understand the meaning of homesickness. My mother tries to make him understand how my sister is feeling – it's tough, she's all on her own, the other girls are mean. And then my grandfather says, simply: 'But we're immigrants.' As if that explained everything. As if hardship and homesickness and melancholy and longing would always be a normal part of our lives. As if we had no reasonable expectation for things to be different. In his easy acceptance of what he saw as his fate – just as my father had accepted his childhood – I suddenly saw how I would never truly be able to communicate with him, this kind, gentle man whose blood I had inherited, whose culture I had absorbed without question. Not even when I was older, and had travelled and learnt about the world and its joys and sadness, maybe even experienced a tiny bit of what he had in his lifetime. The impossibility of any convergence between our respective positions became clear in that brief moment. He was an immigrant. I was a grandchild of an immigrant. We would never see the world in the same way.

II

Swee Ee

or

Eternity

We thought we would find you dead, but instead you are sitting next to me, more alive than ever.

Two weeks prior to this, my parents and I had driven from Kuala Lumpur to see you, more than three hours through heavy traffic until we reached the small rural town where you have lived for nearly sixty years, and where I spent all my school holidays with you. You were very sick by then; the cancer had spread so extensively that no one was sure which part of your body was causing you the most pain. I spent half an hour with you, sitting by your bed while you slept. Your lips were cracked and you had lost so much weight that your cheeks had collapsed to the bone. You had never been a tall person but now, motionless in bed, you looked like a child. My mother spent only a few minutes with you. What's the point, she said, your grandmother doesn't even know we're here. Much later, she would admit to me that she couldn't bear the sight of you on the threshold of death. There was no air in the room; she found it hard to breathe.

Last night I was preparing to leave the country – a book tour and other work commitments that would keep me away for several months – when Uncle C rang, very late, to say you were slipping away. It wasn't worth coming, he said; he just wanted to let us know. But we drove back anyway, to begin the funeral arrangements and spend a few days sorting through your affairs. There would be strange lightness in the mood of the house, the melancholy shot through with a sense of relief at your passing, just as we had experienced two decades earlier when Ah Gong had died, and you had said yourself, At least he's not in pain anymore.

We pulled into the back lane that always smells of chicken shit, and I remembered the sensation of loneliness I always experienced as a child when I came to stay with you for the school holidays, away from my life in the city. I wish I could speak fondly of the nostalgia of returning to the family village, but it was never the case with me. Uncle C was waiting for us out in the lane, shielding his eyes against the midday sun. Something strange is happening, he said. We walked into the kitchen and saw you standing by the kettle, waiting for it to come to the boil. You had a towel around your neck, your hair, always curly and dyed black, was freshly washed and you'd put on a new blouse and a pair of dark trousers. You tried to lift the kettle but didn't quite have the strength; the effort made your legs tremble. It was as if you hadn't noticed that your body was failing you.

Uncle C whispered, It's been weeks since she's been able to stand up.

You looked up and saw us standing there. *Come, come*, you said, calling me by my childhood nickname, you must be thirsty, Granny make you some tea. You referred to yourself in the third person, just as you always had. It was as if we'd seen each other every week for the last three decades – as if there was no gulf between us.

You took me through to the sitting room and sat next to me on the plastic-covered sofa. Your eyes were bloodshot and tired but you were still eager for company. I could hear my parents talking in low, urgent tones with Uncle C in the next room, but I couldn't make out what they were saying because I was concentrating on your voice.

It is this moment – both too short and somehow eternal – that comes back to me from time to time these days, when I am waiting for a bus or about to fall asleep. You are talking to me, your face beaming with the pleasure of being alive even though you know that you are dying. You are speaking with a freedom I have never seen in you, telling me things about my grandfather, about yourself, incidents which even my mother will not be familiar with. It's because you're so close to Granny, she will say later, but in fact it is the opposite. You're telling me these things because we have grown apart, and sometimes it's easier to be intimate with a stranger.

Alone with you, in what we both know will be our last

conversation, it strikes me that the story of our relationship is the story of separation.

Our closeness is measured in the distance between us.

*

When I was at university in Britain, I found myself talking to a fellow student, a willowy blonde boy from an old, grand family, who was summarising his genealogy. Only *one* part of my family is aristocratic, he laughed, the other part is just nineteenth-century industrial money. I listened carefully as he patiently explained the hierarchy of dukes, marquesses, earls and so on. I was new to the country and fascinated by people's interest in social backgrounds – fascinated, also, by the way the British were able to make this interest seem so casual that any curiosity about family circumstances felt almost incidental, ancillary to politeness.

It was lunchtime. Other students joined us, setting down their trays on the long refectory tables and slipping easily into the conversation about families and lineage while they ate a curious dish that I remember clearly, *Chicken à la King* (British eating habits, which seemed impossibly complex and exotic, were another of my early fascinations with the country: if dinner was sometimes tea, when was tea? Why was tea sometimes finger sandwiches, sometimes chips and egg? Was supper the same as dinner? It certainly wasn't the same as the *siew-ye* we had back in Malaysia. I was also mystified by the question of education – why were private schools called *public*? – the terminology of toilets, plastic basins in kitchen sinks, and so on.)

I'm always *really* surprised, the blonde boy said, when people don't know the maiden names of their four great-grandmothers. He was teased by the others for being 'posh', but they nonetheless rose to the challenge and managed to dredge up one or two of their great-grandmothers' names, or at least a few salient facts of their lives – one the daughter of a Galician sailor caught in a storm and swept all the way to Wales; another a shepherdess in Cumbria; someone else a seamstress of lace, some pieces of which had been handed down all the way to her great-grandchildren. One great-grandmother had had an affair with a French count whose father had been the inspiration for a minor character in *In Search of Lost Time*.

I kept silent and laughed, as if it was all a joke, to hide the fact that I was thinking of you; to hide the awkwardness of having no knowledge of who your mother was. Her name had long since been scrubbed from our family's collective memory – our country's too. Of her face, nothing is remembered. The way she laughed, the things that made her happy or enraged, the people she loved, those who oppressed her: nothing has been retained.

It is the same story on the other side of our family, as it is with almost all the friends in Malaysia to whom I ask the question the blonde boy asked me. Who were your great-grandparents? *Must have been labourers from Madras* or *Donno, farmers in Fujian province?* is the most detailed answer I get.

Everything else is lost.

*

No one knows exactly what year you were born in, or where. All we know is that you were born in a remote village, a cluster of wooden houses, deep in the jungle. *Some very ulu place* is how my mother puts it. She deduces the inaccessibility and deprivation of your birthplace from the fact you once told her that when your father died – you were still a small child then – his body had to be transported to the nearest hospital by bullock cart. *Dragged out of the jungle by a gu-chia.*

My mother didn't think to ask where this took place, and you didn't elaborate. Already, you believed that your story was not important. To be born a girl in a poor family early in the twentieth century was to resign yourself to certain facts: you would not be sent to school, you would instead be put to work at the earliest age, you would wait to be married to the first suitable man who came for you, you would have children with him, your life would be less important than that of your family's. Your past, and your present, would give way to their future.

How would you tell your story, anyway, even to those close to you? Once, my sister – still very small, in her early days of school – innocently asked you what your favourite subject was when you were at school. I was still a child too, but old enough to understand the embarrassment of the question. Without you ever having talked about your childhood, I knew that you had not been allowed to go to school; that your intelligence and humour disguised your complete lack of formal education; that the simple act of sitting in a classroom aged six or seven made us different from you.

I can't ever recall you talking about yourself: whether you were happy or sad with a situation in the family or the village – all you discussed was the wellbeing of others. You asked about our homework, whether we were eating well, how our friends were. You wanted our young lives to take centre stage while yours was willingly relegated to the shadows.

One time I came into the shop that the family ran – a modest shop on half of the ground floor of this old shophouse that we're sitting in now. It was one of those quiet times of the day, just after lunch when the afternoon heat was at its fiercest and there was no one in the street. I was going to take up my usual place near the front of the shop, where I looked after the counter selling soap and hairbrushes and shampoo, and the women who travelled in from the jungle villages would occasionally buy something cheap from me, a bar of Popinjay soap or a packet of hairpins, because they found it amusing to purchase something sold by a child from the city. That day you were alone in the shop, talking to a customer who wanted to buy some dishcloths. Her voice was raised. I couldn't hear what she was saying, but her tone was aggressive, the rapidity of her speech suggesting the conversation was more than just about the price. The air was shot with the hissing of air valves from the tyre-repair shop next door. I heard the woman say the word *Cina*, the two syllables dragged long, a sudden, terrible slowing of the rhythm of the sentence, when that single word comes to mean more than just *Chinese*, and the very person you are becomes an insult.

You kept smiling, making calming noises, ya okay, *okaaay*, as you folded up the towels neatly and placed them back into the cabinet. I came and stood next to you and asked if you were alright. You smiled and said, I'm used to it, I learned to deal with lots of angry customers where I worked when I was young.

Where was that?

In a place in Ipoh.

I couldn't think of a way to ask more questions about your work and what it had meant to you. The time didn't seem right – has never felt right. The way you smiled made me feel more hurt than relief, and I couldn't understand why.

*

By the end of my first year in Britain I felt I'd deciphered most of the basic codes of everyday life. I had learnt that when asked how I was, the correct response was not that

I was homesick, or miserable because of the low skies and drizzle, and maybe battling depression, but that I was *fine*. That wasn't difficult to work out, being the rough equivalent of the Asian way of greeting someone by asking them whether they had eaten lunch or dinner, the answer always being, yes, or just about to – an exchange that expressed concern without any real concern.

At university the students drank until last orders and explained to me how to consume entire pints of beer as pub closing time approached. *Just open your gullet and pour it down.* The next morning the men would be absent from lectures, emerging from their rooms only at lunchtime or even later in the afternoon with bloodshot eyes, but at the end of the year they would perform superbly in exams, announcing their results as casually as possible, as if they were at once accidental and inevitable. *Um yeah, I got a first?* What I discovered was that after leaving the pub, they dozed off the alcohol before working intensely in the quiet hours of the morning. I learned that the quality they prized was effortless brilliance; to be too serious or too committed was not to be admired. This studied nonchalance was the diametric opposite of everything I had known and valued throughout an upbringing in which an overt engagement with achievement was the cornerstone of collective and individual social progress. Still, this obliqueness wasn't so hard to figure out. Growing up in an ethnic Chinese family in Malaysia, I'd learnt what minorities everywhere absorb by instinct: you have to prove that you're hardworking and valuable to society, but not so much that you become a threat, so you deflect attention away from yourself. Self-deprecation was the key to your survival.

What was the difference between self-deprecation and dishonesty? Maybe there wasn't any.

I learned how to discern signs of social capital, which involved inverting most habits I understood. A worn collar, or a jumper with little holes in it, or a general oldness of clothes, which at home would have been considered a shameful indication of poverty, here represented the opposite, not just an advertisement of wealth but *old* wealth. This boundary between deceit and discretion made sense to me. It spoke of a certain silence, and I knew all about that.

*

I am seventeen, sitting in the shop, reading, making notes. I'm supposed to be serving customers but not many people are around, and when someone does come in I barely look up, allowing them to wander around before drifting out again. I've become a surly teenager, trapped by my own concerns with little interest in what happens to others. For a long time I've been lacklustre at school but in the last year or so I have started to feel an urgency linked not so much to studies, but to the idea of escape and reinvention, of leading a totally different kind of life from the one I'm meant to have. I'm not so interested in books and studying but I realise that they are a means to this end, the only solution I can think of to transform my life into something different. You come into the shop and ask, What are you studying? I show you the cover and continue reading.

What is it about? you ask. You smell fresh; it's hot, and you've just patted your neck with more prickly heat powder.

A king, I say after a while. A king who doesn't recognise the daughter who loves him until it's too late.

Ha, why?

I shrug. Because she doesn't tell him.

The truth is, I don't say more because I cannot understand the book, I don't even know what half the words on the page mean, I can't figure out the sentences. Twenty years later I will teach classes and give talks about writing and literature, and people – mostly westerners – will ask me questions about the absorption of colonial mentality, why I write in the white man's language, and I will consider issues of the dominant and the enslaved, the white gaze, the celebration of the vernacular, of subaltern cultures; and sometimes I will think of you, and wonder how you fit into all of this.

Like the time in Australia when, after one of my readings, a well-meaning man with strawberry-blonde hair, wearing Thai fisherman trousers and a Chinese-y shirt, stands up and starts his question with *apa khabar* and then asks if I choose to write in English because it sells better, and whether I feel a victim of western capitalist market forces. Or is it because I have a *colonised mind*? (I will smile and think of you).

All that is for much later. Right now I am concentrating

61

on deciphering the words on the page in front of me. There is so much that is impenetrable, but I understand one line instinctively and profoundly:

Love, and be silent.

*

After your father died, you were sent to live with your aunt in Ipoh. (Your mother had already passed away, shortly after giving birth to your youngest brother. Hers is another life that goes unrecorded, lost now, despite all attempts to find out about her – not only do I not know her maiden name, I can't find anyone who knows a single fact about her. How old she was when she died; even her name. *Poor people, that's how it is.* That's the sentence I hear, translated from Hokkien or Cantonese, so often that I no longer ask questions.)

You were sent to work – selling raffle tickets, cleaning the floor in a canteen, a variety of menial jobs. But you were clever, everyone could see that, and as you grew older you were given more important jobs like counting the day's takings, even some bookkeeping. You were good with people, always cheerful, customers liked you wherever you worked. Throughout your teens you gave your earnings to your aunt, to support your younger brothers and probably her children too, all of you living under one roof. You enjoyed going out, but opportunities were limited. When you weren't working to earn money, you were working to run the household – the fate of an orphaned girl like you was to be at the mercy of others.

There were young men on the horizon, boys who'd take you for a stroll around the old town in Ipoh; hand-holding, a bit of *pak-torh*, vague promises of marriage. How could there not be? You were bright, pretty, unfailingly cheerful. A woman of your generation in Asia is not supposed to have a romantic life before marriage, not a public one, anyway. Whatever may have happened in private – with men or women – has to be erased in favour of the official story of marital love; it is marriage that validates your existence and makes you visible to the world. It would be the same for my mother's generation too, and maybe even now. Occasionally, eavesdropping on my father's conversations with his buddies, I hear jokes about ex-girlfriends in Kota Bharu or Kuala Krai; but never any mention of ex-boyfriends in my mother's circle of friends.

Yet in this too-brief moment we are sharing, you say, *I already had a happy life before marrying your Ah Gong.* Your eyes are shining with a quiet brilliance as you speak, even though your body is so weak that you tremble slightly and have to grip the armrest to steady yourself.

You had a boyfriend, but your aunt didn't approve of the relationship – less because of the young man himself, but because she couldn't afford your departure from the household. The money you earned paid for food and your younger brothers' schooling, and on top of that you were a hard worker, you had so much stamina for someone so small. You cleaned the house, did the washing, prepared meals, kept things going. The boyfriend wasn't rich enough to pay a dowry that would compensate for your aunt's loss of you. In provincial Malaysia at the end of the 1940s, everyone could see that you were worth more than what you were on paper: the orphan of a destitute peasant.

The Second World War had just ended, and life in small-town Malaysia was picking up again. You wouldn't know that thousands of miles away, civil servants in Whitehall were contemplating Britain's bankruptcy after its wartime campaigns. The old British Empire was fracturing, but the Federation of Malaya was still the world's biggest producer of tin and rubber, crucial to British revenues and its efforts to rebuild itself. All that tinned food during the long years of rationing and prudence in mid-century Britain was made possible by the men and women who worked in the region where you lived, who came to eat every day in the canteen where you worked. The tin miners, the middlemen, the printers, fruit growers, the sausage-makers; the people who surrounded you as you became an adult.

But even your aunt couldn't ignore the fact that you had been of marriageable age for some time, and soon you would be too old to be married off in exchange for a dowry. That's how life was back then, you say. *What to do?* You laugh, and in that little moment of levity I sense how aware you were of your predicament. A young woman with a full life watching on as the world decided her fate for her.

*

How can I remember you and still be modern? I once wrote a novel populated with characters of your generation, people who could have been you. They lived through the war and did what they needed to survive, just as you did. The novel sold many copies and was widely talked about; young writers started to send their manuscripts to publishers. One fashionable editor, based in the capital, wrote in a social media post: *We're not interested in your grandmother's stories about the war, or the shoes she had when she was young.*

This is what it means to be modern in Asia today: you are required to detach yourself from the past and live only in the present, without considering the people who shaped you. To remember is to be nostalgic, or, even worse, colonised. To write about your heritage and all the elements that make you and the society you live in different – and complicated and sometimes painful – is to be weak.

The irony is actually that, until today, you've never spoken to me about your past in a meaningful way. People of my generation in Asia have always understood that we will have to live with the deep silence that surrounds your generation, and even that of my parents', and that we will not be part of any collective processing of historical trauma. You and I have long ago established an understanding that there will be a break with the past: I work hard and make my life representative of ours; your sorrows disappear from the page, and your joys too.

Some time ago an excerpt from the opening passages of this book was published in a famous American journal. I suggested to my mother, who normally doesn't read my books, that she might like to read the pages in question, seeing as they were about her father. Some days later she rang and said *it was good*, but that I got one detail wrong. When I said that my grandfather had travelled to Malaysia under hazardous circumstances, all on his own, I was mistaken.

There had been another boy from my grandfather's village in Fujian province, and the two teenagers had travelled to Malaysia together. My mother knew this because one day the family received a call from Tanjung Rambutan, the infamous local psychiatric hospital, regarding a patient who was very sick. He had no family and was found wandering the streets of Ipoh. The only name he had was my grandfather's. Would he take him in? There followed angry disputes at home, recounts my mother. Don't let that man come into this house, some members of the family argued, he will bring bad luck on us. But my grandfather insisted. It was his duty; he couldn't abandon his childhood friend, even though they hadn't been in touch for decades.

The man arrived and sat quietly in a chair for three days, caught in a silent, lonely world. He didn't respond to conversation but took meals politely, on his own. He seemed happy just to be on the fringes of what was now a bustling household. On the fourth day he killed himself by drowning in the river at the end of the lane.

There was a long pause on the line. Then my mother said, So, what are you going to have for dinner this evening?

I described the meal I was preparing, something ordinary,

I can't remember what. She asked for more details – what kind of vegetables, what kind of fish – and I supplied the answers. I couldn't find a way to ask anything else.

Some days later, when I had worked through the worst of my frustration at my own inability to communicate, I contemplated ringing my mother to ask why she had never told me about that episode. Already, I could feel myself colluding in the burying of that story. I had so much work going on, I had fun dinners with friends that week, I was moving into a new apartment; yet I couldn't concentrate on anything. That man's life spoke of the death of ambition, the rootlessness of the immigrant, of chance, of loneliness. I had to scrub him from my thoughts if I were to enjoy my own life. I could feel myself letting go of the details of the story, wanting it to become blurry and unthreatening, less real.

Before my nerve failed me, I rang my mother and asked, why.

She said, *Aiya, so boring, what is there to tell?*

*

For all their apparent reserve, people in Britain still occasionally retained the ability to unsettle me, particularly when they spoke about their families. Some fellow students – solidly middle-class as far as I could tell – grumbled about having to pay their parents rent during their gap years before going up to university, a commercial transaction that seemed cold and ruthless to me. I had to pretend that I found it entirely natural that parents could also be landlords in an arrangement where kinship became calculated and calmly adversarial; where reductions in rent (of the bedroom one had occupied since childhood) might be traded against the performing of household chores.

Once, I was chatting with a few friends, including another Malaysian I'd met at the check-in counter at Subang airport, and with whom I'd remained friends ever since. Another friend was speaking, a white British woman from Dulwich, thinking aloud about her complicated relationship with her parents. All the time she was growing up, she had believed the relationship was totally normal, but now she realised it wasn't. Her parents hadn't let her go out much with friends; they loved her, they'd said, and wanted to protect her. Her brother, older and freer, was able to live his life as he pleased, with parental support when he needed it. It's not as though her parents were easy on him or anything, it's just that she always remembered them speaking to him as an adult, giving him choices, consulting him on his opinions. It was only recently, with the help of therapy, that she'd come to realise the obvious: her father loved her *too much*, her mother didn't love her *at all*. She was an adult now, she didn't need her mother's love, but still, a part of her craved it. She was just now realising, she said, that her mother had emotion-ally *fucked her up*.

Everyone made supportive noises but I didn't know what to say. We had known each other for less than a year, and

I wasn't sure how to react. I looked across at my Malaysian friend, and she – someone I thought of as extrovert and daring back home – looked at her mug of tea. We were bound together by our shared awkwardness, both of us at once transfixed and terrified by this frank revelation of family relationships, our discomfort caused by this implicit, forced confrontation of how we communicated within our own families. Braver than I was, she finally said, But it's your mum you're talking about.

Our friend laughed and shrugged. Yeah, like I said, it's fucked up.

Walking back to our lodgings later, my Malaysian friend and I tried to dismiss our momentary embarrassment by defining it as cultural differences. That's Western culture for you, we reassured each other; we have different ways of communicating in Asia.

*

A matchmaker was hired. A few meetings were arranged, but you were judged to be too old or too forthright, too quick to speak your mind. The men you met were sons of country folk, uneducated and lacking your speed of thought, your subtle intelligence. They spoke Chinese dialects, some Malay, no English. You'd worked for years in that canteen, spoken every day with people who spoke every language in the Federated States, rich merchants from Kuala Lumpur and Singapore, even British civil servants. You picked up these languages, you learned to speak English. This made you seem terrifying to the simple boys you met, themselves struggling to find a match. You were too direct, too funny, too stubborn, too unpredictable. You knew what you wanted.

Why can't you just pick someone and get married, your aunt asked. Soon no one will marry you, you will be old and withered, a *ma che*, *laochunü*. Because, you replied. Because I don't care.

The proposals started to dry up; the matchmaker cast the net wider still, and eventually a man was suggested. An older man, a widower whose wife had recently died from tuberculosis. He needed to find a woman who could be a good mother to his two small daughters; someone young and fit enough to give him the son and heir he wanted. He was not an exciting man, not young or handsome or even very rich, but he was kind and decent and steady in temperament. He owned a modest business, a general store in a rural town on the banks of the great river that cuts through the region. He spoke Hokkien, your dialect. He was offering a dowry, nothing spectacular, but acceptable to your aunt. You would soon get married and move into the living quarters above the shop on the main street of the town.

Among your qualities listed by the matchmaker, the principal one was that you were a *strong worker*, an attribute that I still hear today, describing women from struggling families, or who get married in rural areas, including among my own relatives. *Education level not high but she's a strong worker*. This refers to a physical as well as emotional resilience, the ability to withstand long hours of labour – cooking, cleaning, looking after your own children and those of relatives less fortunate than yourself, helping your husband with his work – but above all it presumes a natural aptitude for self-sacrifice. A presumption that your own ambitions and desires will be pushed aside, even extinguished, for the sake of your new family. Whatever satisfaction you might experience will be derived precisely from this lack of personal joy: you have to find happiness in the absence of happiness. You would draw solace from the Chinese expression *chi ku*, to *eat bitterness*, because to suffer is to be admired; that is how the underprivileged justify the harshness of their lives, by turning it into a virtue. In time you'll find yourself saying of someone: she's had a hard life. It sounds like pity, but is intended as a compliment.

Except that was not the story you created. You followed the script but edited it in your own manner. To be in your presence was to feel a sort of lightness, a temporary suspension of worry. You refused to be the resented, resentful stepmother, stepping into someone else's shoes. You gave the home a new energy, your long years of keeping your aunt's home and looking after your brothers made this new life seem easy to you. You reorganised the little shop that your husband had struggled to build, and suddenly business picked up, people liked coming into the shop and chatting with you. Before your arrival the place had been grim, too dark and presided over by my grandfather, who spoke little, his shyness interpreted as severity. You were more fluent, in Cantonese and Malay and English, you drew people towards you. You raised the girls as though they were your own, sent them to school, gave them the opportunities you were deprived of. Whereas life for him and his daughters had felt like a perpetual battle, now it seemed hopeful.

*

In my first long summer vacation at university I took the coach to France, which I'd never visited before. On a thin strip of beach south of Montpellier, I ate yoghurt-flavoured ice cream, drank *panaché* and dozed in the sun. All around me there were families on vacation, the parents calm and sleepy, watching their kids play on the water's edge. They were tanned and loose-limbed, these eternal children, building trenches in the sand or jumping over the low waves that broke on the shore. Even the older ones, pairing up with a tentative girl- or boyfriend, seemed touched with a childlike lightness in that never-ending summer.

In Paris there was a demonstration by high school students. I sat in a café listening to people shouting through loudspeakers, blowing whistles, chanting. I asked the waiter what the protest was about and he simply raised his shoulders, elbows flaring softly for a second. It's France, he said, there are always protests. Later, walking abreast of the crowd I saw the students' faces, shiny with elation and a kind of boldness that was foreign to me, an unshakeable confidence of youth and belonging – of people keenly aware that they were young, and that they could shape the country that belonged to them. I was barely older than they were but their energy and power made me feel sad – and though I couldn't say exactly what I was sad about, I knew it was something to do with being old before my years, and silent.

*

There was also the question of your emotional life. Of love. Your marriage was arranged but it didn't stop you from seeing it as more than a mere transaction – from expecting more of it than just security. You wanted a partner, someone with whom you could laugh, but often you didn't know what to do with this kind, taciturn man who couldn't communicate how he felt, and who found it difficult to keep up with the speed of your thoughts. You didn't know if he appreciated your gaiety or your strong-mindedness, which led the rest of the family to call you *stubborn*. Sometimes you thought that you should be more reserved and acquiescent, the way other women of your age were, but you couldn't help yourself – your cheeriness, your refusal to give way in arguments. *What to do?*

And then, the matter of physical intimacy. You were supposed to have no expectations but you did; you wanted to give and receive affection. You knew, also, that your husband wanted a son to take over the business – you knew

73

that no matter how much he loved his daughters, only a son would do. How long did it take you to find out what your husband had lived through before you married him? To discover that he had been tortured during the war, as so many ethnic Chinese men had been in rural areas, and now he *could no longer have children*. How much frustration did you both have to endure in order to realise his impotence, which maybe explained his timidity, and his occasional bouts of fragility. His digestive system would be weak for the rest of his life, his kidneys too, and you would feel a curious sense of superiority over him, an uncomfortable sensation that you would be aware of for the rest of your life, despite trying to ignore it.

You would take care to make your intelligence less obvious when you were with him, especially in the presence of others; you wouldn't talk about all the things you read about in the papers, would restrain yourself whenever you felt you'd offered an opinion that went too far. You'd recognise that people were drawn more easily to you than him, especially your grandchildren, and you'd be careful to share that affection equally, encouraging the little ones to spend time with him, separately, when really they would have chosen to be entirely in your company. You'd remind them that he loved them despite his silence. *You know old people like your Ah Gong, they don't know how to talk about such things*, you'd say, laughing.

*

There came a point at university when everyone started to think about jobs. Employers from London sent their representatives to recruit eager students, and each day the post room was filled with an air of anticipation as some people received offers of employment while others continued to wait. Over lunch people would mention their post-graduation jobs with an exaggerated reticence that was the equivalent of boasting. *I'm going to Morgan Stanley?* people would say, almost as if they had forgotten how their lucrative employment had occurred.

One group of people fascinated me above all others – the ones who shrugged and announced that they were going to be writers. I'll probably just move to London to finish my novel, they said. The process of *just moving* seemed to me fraught with obstacles, none of which appeared to trouble these young men and women, already fully formed in their writerly identities. Foremost among the list of barriers was the absence of a job, and the consequent lack of money. How could I rent a flat if I had no money? Then, the alchemy of publishing a novel, before stitching together a career as a writer. Nothing was said about what happened after that novel was finished. How did *just moving* to London translate into becoming Margaret Atwood? It would be some time before I worked out that many of these young writers had parents who were lawyers or university lecturers, or even successful writers themselves. Complex as it might have been, *just moving* to London and publishing a novel was a process that they would somehow work out, drawing from a vast well of collective experience that remained foreign to me. At that time, all I could hear was my parents' voices, urgently asking, *have you got a job yet?*

I needed to figure out ways to mould my desire to write into that magical state of becoming a writer, so I attended a workshop, led by a well-known writer. Here is some of the advice I scribbled down that day, in a notebook I am soon going to consign to the recycling bin:

Never be direct or obvious.

No one is interested in misery memoirs.

If you have to write about trauma, try being oblique – maybe use an animal narrator, or an inanimate object like a chair?

*

As you grew older you took less care in hiding your moments of private pleasure, and we would often find you watching wrestling matches on TV while sipping a large tumbler of whisky, filled so full that it looked as if you were drinking tea, which is what we told the younger grandchildren, though even they knew it wasn't true. We are not talking about elegant Greco-Roman *lutte*: what you liked was the extravagant theatricality of Randy Savage, André the Giant, Jake the Snake and the young Hulk Hogan. Your grandchildren gathered around you as you chuckled and cheered with each body-slam and fake kick to the head, which you insisted were real, despite our protests. Who knows why you loved the spectacle of all that long gelled hair, buff muscle and exaggerated male violence? You never got drunk, never even suffered from a flushed face like the rest of the family did if ever they drank too much alcohol; you merely sat giggling quietly, as if regaining an innocence that you had lost too early.

In those moments I recognised myself in you and saw how I might be when I was your age, both of us trying to make up for a childhood we had surrendered prematurely to responsibility and worry.

As you speak to me now, with barely a pause between your sentences, I realise that this is something we share: a feeling of always making up for lost time. Except, there is never enough time.

*

All these poor suffering Asians, I'm so fed up of them! That's what a white British person once said over a dinner party, *jokingly*, of course.

I know, right? I'm tired of them too! I said, not joking at all. I'm tired of having to drag around this story that is mine. I wish my history was filled with more colourful detail, that I could talk about great-great-grandparents who led war campaigns in foreign lands and came back with treasures and trophies that adorn my living room. Who lived in one place – one village in one country – all their lives, and if ever they travelled to build bridges or railways on the other side of the world they would always return to that bucolic hamlet, where there would be monuments inscribed with their names.

But that is not what I have. I have you. You are my history. You are my past and my present, and I will talk about you.

*

Stories. Histories. I must learn more, know more, understand more, analyse more, theorise more. More more more.

This is the world I live in now. I have come to equate knowing with living, and I want to live. You have to tell me everything. Time is slipping away from us. Stay with me.

We have to make things last forever.

*

One cultural habit I discovered with relish in Britain was what people called *a walk*. I had grown up with temperatures hovering constantly around the thirty-degree mark, accompanied by humidity levels so high that rain always seemed ready to burst from the skies. In such conditions, walking was rarely something to look forward to, whether for pleasure or out of necessity – the only people who did so were old men who strolled around the neighbourhood in the early evening, dressed in thin white singlets.

On my first walk in Britain, on a weekend staying with the family of a friend in the country (what was the difference between 'country' and 'countryside'?), I expected a similarly gentle circuit, in this case through a pastoral setting of wheat fields and meadows dotted with sheep grazing lazily. It turned out to be a brisk march that lasted nearly two hours, the pace never faltering where the paths turned to mud or became shrouded with bramble. My hosts ran into friends from neighbouring villages, themselves out for a walk – we were all miles from any visible dwelling – and discussed meeting the following week for lunch, or dinner, or maybe tea on Sunday. After much debate, someone suggested, *Why don't we go for a walk?* That was the obvious solution, the proposal was delivered with such earnestness that made it impossible to agree to anything less. Coffee, drinks, a meal – none of those carried the moral quality of a walk, which also promised a reward of a pint or two or even lunch in a pub afterwards, the hedonism of that moment well deserved following the physical activity of the walk.

Once, I found myself walking in Gloucestershire with a friend who'd invited some other people to join the party. It was a post-lunch ramble with no destination in mind. The footpaths skirted along the edges of freshly tilled fields, the rich smell of earth drifted in the air. Occasionally the path would take us through a picturesque village with a stone bridge over a stream or a little church nestled among trees. A vista would open up, revealing a broad shoulder of a hill, the fields divided into neat parcels. People made appreciative noises at such moments, and eventually one man – born in the Southwest of the country but for many years a lawyer in the City – said, I know it sounds weird, but at a time like this I really feel *attached* to the land. He stopped and admired the view, genuinely moved by what he saw. I know it's really sentimental, but I do feel that I belong here. I feel that all this is . . . I mean . . . *this belongs to me.*

Oh for goodness' sake, I'm going to throw up, someone else teased, but no amount of ribbing could deny the man's sincerity. I felt caught up in his rootedness, vicariously experiencing his unshakeable sense of belonging, and suddenly the landscape was not only pretty, it made sense to me as a place of stability and security.

It wasn't until some days later, back in London, that I thought about my own attachment to the Malaysian land-scape – to the Malaysian *country*. I was in my teens when I learned that, as ethnic Chinese citizens, we did not have the legal right to own certain kinds of land, vast tracts of prime forest or real estate. Wrong race, wrong religion. We didn't think of ourselves as immigrants – very few immi-grants do – but here was a reminder. We could possess the nationality, but we couldn't fully possess the earth.

Still, there are laws, and there is your relationship with the *tanah air*, the soil you stand on.

*

Sometimes when I type *love*, my phone changes the word to *live*. Several times in my notes for this book, typed quickly on a bus or a train, I have the line *Live, and be silent*.

A few months ago I saw a documentary made by a Malaysian filmmaker, Tham Seen Hau, about her mother, who grew up in a family of ten that lived in a modest part of Kuala Lumpur when the race riots broke out on 13 May 1969. Among the hundreds of ethnic Chinese citizens who were killed that day were five members of the family. From the very next day, the surviving five never again talked about the murder of their kin. Not once in fifty years have they mentioned the savagery inflicted upon them. For decades they have continued to live within a few miles of each other, but rarely get in touch.

Recently, the cemetery in which the family and other victims of the massacre are buried was earmarked to be destroyed in order to build a new car park. The city is expanding and modernising, we all have cars now, we need more space. The stories of the victims have already been lost – their faces, their personalities, the way they laughed, the food they liked to eat, what exactly happened to them on that terrible day. Soon their names, too, will be gone. As one of the survivors says in the film, they will be merely a number, one of a few hundred people killed that day.

Why dig up past troubles? Seen Hau was asked when she suggested making a film commemorating this trauma. We have to live in the modern world. Neither victim nor aggressor wants to be reminded of our conflicts – our weaknesses, our aggression. We don't want to be defined by the way society has failed us, by the way we have failed others. We have to look only to the future.

I understand this. I really do.

But still.

*

Some lessons I wish you'd taught me:

Immigrants are meant to declare, constantly and loudly, their love for their country. Not to do so is an act of treachery and ingratitude. In this instance, your love, which is elsewhere complex and wordless, must be performative; the theatricality makes everyone feel better.

You must say out loud, from time to time, I'm proud to be Malaysian/British/American/whatever. Even better if you can muster a full sentence like, I know there are problems in this country but honestly, compared to China/Pakistan/Nigeria/wherever, life here is so good. This applies even if you've never lived in any other country – even if you were born in your country, of parents who were born in that country, and have no experience of life in India, China, Vietnam etc.

In fact: the earlier you think of yourself as an immigrant, the better. It avoids the confusion you'll experience when you first hear people telling you to go back to X/Y/Z country. The only problem is, it will be impossible for you to feel that you're an immigrant – that is something others describe you as. You feel you belong, entirely, to that country, and it to you. Even when, older and more culturally connected, you want to reclaim your other identities, travel to the country of your ancestors, visit the harbour from which they sailed to the new-found land, it will feel a bit hollow, a bit of a performance (in any case the harbour is now a giant port full of tankers and container ships, and when you speak the language you learned from your parents and grandparents, the people there find the way you talk cute, as if you've stepped out of a black and white movie). Immigrant, foreigner – and any variation of that notion, as reflected in the words you'll hear – is a state of being you never fully recognise in yourself.

You knew all this, but whether by instinct or choice, you chose not to transmit any of this to me. You conspired, with my parents, to shield me from all of this, you nurtured this attachment I have to the land, so silent and easy that it doesn't even feel like love but something more primal, like oxygen, that I inhale and synthesise and add to the collective air simply by existing. You said, when someone first called me *Cina babi* and I actually wondered whether the Chinese were pigs because we ate pork, or because of some deeper reason I wasn't yet aware of – because I was only six, and how could I know – you said, It's nothing. You laughed and said, they're just kids, they don't know what they're saying. Your words made the confusion fade away swiftly. In my mind I saw and heard a couple of children, young and stupid as you said, completely unthreatening. That was how I shrugged off the insult every time I heard it in the future.

In fact, that first time, they were not kids. It was adults who said that. I never corrected you then; I'm telling you now.

Soon after, when I first heard *balik Tongsan*, I honestly thought it was aimed at someone other than me, a random passer-by from Beijing. That's why they had to go back to China. Their holiday was over, their flight was leaving, they had to return. That's how a child's mind works, it protects itself by inventing different realities, but sometimes those stories are too fragile to stand up to scrutiny, and I told you what had been said to me. Then, again, you conspired to shelter me. *Aiya, go back where*, you laughed. *How to go, can sit bus go back to China meh?* You made it seem ridiculous, a notion so illogical and fantastical that it couldn't exist. Yet you and I both knew that the insult was real, and that you had heard it many times before. (You were too casual, too quick to miscomprehend.) We stood in the kitchen laughing. You gave me a glass of sweet barley water and said, Let's go to Pusing tonight to eat noodles, I'll treat you to your favourite Hokkien Mee.

In those moments, I knew that your denial of the insult was a form of protection; your silence was an expression of love.

*

One July afternoon in Athens last year, when the sun was so hot it appeared white, I got bored of reading and went out for a walk with no destination in mind. I walked slowly, hugging the shady side of the pavements to keep cool, and tried to take note of the changing of street names as I moved from one neighbourhood to another. I'm entirely at ease in hot weather, but that day, even I began to struggle. It was a mistake to venture out at that time of the day, and as I made my way along the marble pedestrianised road that traces the contours of the Acropolis I began to feel dizzy. I sat in the shade of a tree, on a low stone bench, and watched the people go by. There were a fair number of tourists about despite the heat, including groups of well-heeled visitors from China striking film-star poses with the Parthenon rising in the distance behind them. The women looked unbothered by the heat in their airy white dresses and huge floppy sunhats, the men in cargo shorts and wraparound sunglasses.

A group of three or four Chinese vendors darted among their wealthier compatriots, offering battery-powered fans and plastic sun-visors for sale at just one or two euros. Who knew how long these vendors had been in the country, or what their future was? For that summer, at least, selling cheap little plastic goods to tourists was their entire life.

After a while, when the main group of tourists had dispersed, one of the vendors came and sat in the shade not far from me. She turned on a handheld fan and brought it to her chin, closing her eyes. When she took off her hat I could see her hair was more grey than black. She reached into her pocket and took out a fistful of White Rabbit candy, unwrapping each one carefully and staring into the distance as she savoured the sweetness. *Auntie*, I said, are you sure it's safe to eat those? There's melamine in them.

She laughed as she stood up. That was in the past, now it's made with milk from New Zealand. Look it up online. She chuckled as she put her hat on. Young people nowadays, you worry about *everything*.

She had spotted a new cluster of tourists coming down the hill and slung her bag over her shoulder. Just before she left our shared pool of shade she turned and offered me a portable fan. Only two euros, she said. I took it and fumbled in my pocket for change, but before I could draw out the money she said, Don't bother, just take it.

Then she was off, walking so briskly she almost broke into a run.

*

The precise time is hard to pinpoint, but we got our first colour TV at the end of 1983, so it must be a year or so afterwards that this takes place: I'm sitting in front of the TV, which I watch at every opportunity, even though my parents shout at me to turn it off, not because they are concerned about our eyesight or that they would prefer us to be studying, but because they are afraid that excessive use of the TV will ruin it and they can't afford a new one. On this occasion I stumble across an American singer. Later, I will find out he is called *Prince*, but at this point in time I don't even know why or how he is on Malaysian TV – a mass of long hair and furious, unpredictable energy as he flings himself around a mike stand. He wears a thin moustache *and* eyeshadow and mascara *and* a flowing red chiffon scarf, a heady, unfamiliar mixture of masculine and feminine which, years later, with new vocabulary, I will learn to describe as gender non-conforming, or in some way Queer, but at this moment I am merely transfixed, I am beginning to think about the way I want to live the rest of my life. You come into the room and stand next to me, looking at the TV. Neither of us can really make out what the singer is singing in his rapid falsetto but we both know it is something most parents of this time and place would consider *inappropriate* due to the myriad reasons at once undefined and clearly understood in conventional Asian families. Maybe it is his physical appearance, his lack of masculinity, which amount to a lack of respect (to what, to whom?), an insult to social norms the way Leslie Cheung and his silver shoulder pads are in *Monica*, which is also on TV screens around this time. I wait for you to say something disapproving, or even order me to switch the TV off, but you don't, you stand there watching it with me until the song is almost finished.

You smile and say in English, *Very nice!* and walk away, leaving me to contemplate the last images on the screen, swirling and multicoloured, as if obscured by hallucinogenic smoke.

*

I was on a bus in Singapore recently, pulling on my hoodie against the chill of the air-conditioning. The woman in the seat in front of me was looking at the screen of her phone, and although I tried not to look it was impossible not to notice what was going on. There was no one on the screen, just an empty room, though the phone was set to speaker mode and I could hear an adult voice in the distance. A child, a small boy, appeared in the frame, holding a plastic toy of some sort, offering it to the camera before setting it down and playing with it. He was concentrating on the toy and didn't look up; it was as if the woman in the bus didn't exist. The woman said something in Tagalog but the child continued to play, disappearing after several seconds before returning with another toy. I realised that the woman was covering her face to hide the fact she was crying.

I tried to concentrate on my book, but it was impossible

to ignore the woman's voice, even though she was speaking softly. *Mahal ka ni mommy*, she said; and again, more insistently. *Mommy loves you.* The child wasn't listening, he had drifted off camera again.

Stories of parents forced to leave their children in search of work were so much part of my consciousness that I never thought of them as unusual. In fact they weren't even stories, but mere mentions, as if this sort of separation was a universal fact of life. *I was sent to live with my aunt for a few years; we left our baby with my sister for a year or two.* The casual vagueness of these incidental tales, summed up in a quick sentence, is relevant for it speaks not only of the normality of separation, but of the pain that it produces, so deep that it can't be spoken of in any other way than perfunctorily. I never wanted to know how that pain looked, the precise way it carved its shape into the soul; it was so common to me that I could ignore it the way I did with floods in the monsoon season and water shortages in Selangor. Shit happens, and usually in the background to our lives. We look elsewhere, or invent short-form explanations to brush the complexity away. *That's just life, isn't it?*

But on that bus I saw, played out in the starkest terms, how you must have felt – you, my mother, my father, numerous aunts, uncles, cousins – when your parents had to leave you, and when you, in turn, would have to leave your children for many months at a time. When I asked my parents why they left their six-month-old baby with relatives while they looked for work, they mumbled something about having no choice. *We did it so that you would never have to do the same.*

For our family and others like us, separation is an expression of love. Not just in the physical sense, but in the way we think. We want our children to have an education and a job, to experience life in the way we never could, knowing that everything they gain will make them more distant from us. Loving someone means separating yourself from them. The future is lived vicariously through their achievements: their lives must follow an upward trajectory. They must not fail. That is what social mobility means in Asia today.

When I look at you now, frail but strong enough to talk over the high-pitched whistling of your hearing aid, which has never worked very well, I am struck by how all the distance between us has never made us feel closer. I know you can hear me over that infernal mechanical whining. You've always been able to.

The light is fading and you're starting to stumble over your words. You laugh as you recount episodes from my childhood, my misdemeanours and illnesses, things we've all heard many times before. Your eyes are glassy and your voice is hoarse. When you take a sip of water some of it dribbles down your chin, blotting your blouse.

My mother and Uncle C appear. Granny is tired, she should rest now, she's talked enough.

You keep talking to fill the space, but we all know that

time is up. You have to go to sleep now and I must leave, as I always do.

Stay a while more, you say. I'll take you to Pusing, treat you to your favourite Hokkien mee. *Come, I belanja you.*

Next time, Granny. Next time.